Get Out!

OUTDOOR activities KIDS CAN ENJOY everywhere (except indoors)

Hallie Warshaw

with Jake Miller

Photography by Julie Brown

Sterling Publishing Co., Inc.
New York

Get Out!

Creative Director
Hallie Warshaw

Photographer
Julie Brown

Activity Writer
Jake Miller

Supporting Text Writer
Lael Kimble

Contributing Writer
Mark Shulman

Graphic Designer & Illustrator
Madeleine Budnick

Editor
Robyn Brode

Production Artist
Doug Popovich

Creative Assistants
Kris Bhat
Tanya Napier

Photoshoot Assistant
Phyllis Christopher

10 9 8 7 6 5 4 3 2 1

First paperback edition published in 2003 by
Sterling Publishing Company, Inc.
387 Park Avenue South, New York, NY 10016

Created and produced by Orange Avenue, Inc.
599 Third Street Suite 306, San Francisco, CA 94107, USA

Distributed in Canada by Sterling Publishing Co., Inc.
C/o Canadian Manda Group, One Atlantic Avenue, Suite 105
Toronto, Ontario, Canada M6K 3E7

Distributed in Great Britain and Europe by Chris Lloyd
at Orca Book Services, Stanley House, Fleets Lane,
Poole BH15 3AJ, England

Distributed in Australia by Capricorn Link (Australia) Pty Ltd.
P.O. Box 704, Windsor NSW 2756, Australia

Printed in China
All rights reserved

Sterling ISBN 0-8069-9091-0 Hardcover
              1-4027-0169-1 Paperback

Created by

Orange Avenue

Making Creative Products for Growing Minds

San Francisco • New York

If you would like to correspond with us, send an email with your favorite outdoor activities to getout@orangeavenue.com.

THANK YOU

IT TAKES A LOT OF PEOPLE TO MAKE A BOOK!

Many thanks to all those who participated in the creation, execution, and production of this book. We couldn't have done it without all of you!

CHILDREN MODELS

Rachel Marie Babasa-Young
Kaima Beckham
Surya Bhat
Dyantha Burton
Julia Burton
Phillip Burton
Maya Ruth Cameron
Michael Kemper Cameron
Aaron A. K. Carmack
Anthony Carter
Michael Carter

Lea Chernock
Talia Marie Coombes
Aaron Evans
Ryan "Hank" Foo
Blanca Rosa Gutierrez
Luis Alfonso Gutierrez
Zachariah Ho Seher
Zephaniah Ho Seher
Zoe Ho Seher
Ariel Krietzman
Nina Krietzman

Ryan Loera
Keizha Marie Rejano
Gabrielle Rodriguez Fusco
Mario Rodriguez Fusco
Christopher Scally
Tommy Scally
Emiko Shimabukuro
Emma Smart
Emma K. Timboy-Pickering
Adam Wojewidka

PHOTOSHOOT HOMES

Thank you for letting us use your homes: the Calica-Fishbach family, the Ho Seher family, the Johnson family, the Lanier family, and the Van Den Handel family

ADDITIONAL THANKS

Charles Nurnberg, Frances Gilbert, Sheila Barry, Emily Vassos, Connie Johnson, Rosanne Roberts, Bob Warshaw, Maureen Golden, and Cosmo Mendelsohn

Contents

This book will make you wonder why you need those four walls around you at all!

Is the air feeling thin? Are you stuck to the couch? Arms and legs stapled down so you don't fall off? Starting to wonder what those things at the ends of your legs called feet are for? **Pry yourself off the cushions, open the door, and check out that bright yellow orb in the sky.** It won't hurt you, and it sure is bright. Start moving those limbs and see how it feels to get out of the box!

The activities in GET OUT will start your heart racing and make you laugh so hard you'll get out of breath. Wind will blow in your hair, and

you'll get sap on your fingers. All of this, and every once in a while you'll notice just how big the trees are and how colorful the leaves in the grass. You'll touch the earth, make dirt, make paper out of grass, chase your friends across a field . . . having so much fun that your in-the-house life will look flat and two-dimensional. **Did you know that where you hang out the most greatly affects your personality?** If you spend all your time in the house, maybe you'll end up being square! But if you spend lots of time outside, maybe you'll get a nice round head with sky all around it, and your feet will grow roots that make you stand taller and fall down less. The truth is that all living things are happy outside, as long as it's not face-crackingly cold and you don't have to run from dinosaurs. **Let GET OUT take you there with tons of fun activities and new ideas!**

Watch Out!

It's a jungle out there, so be careful. All beasts know the rules of the wild, and if they do what they are told, they don't get eaten. It's a bit like that for you. Keep yourself safe out there, and follow these ten important rules:

1

Be careful what you eat when you're outside. Don't eat something just because it's pretty. There are lots of cool-looking berries, flowers, mushrooms, and grasses outside. But don't put them in your mouth unless someone you know well and trust says it's okay. You don't want to turn green and have your tummy turned inside-out.

2

Wear sunscreen. The sun is beautiful and bright, but if you're out for a long time at the peak of the day, it can kiss your face in a very rude way, leaving big, red, sore spots that hurt.

3

Stay away from the street. That's where the biggest beasts run on dinosaur juice and come roaring through at high speeds. Any animal will tell you this is bad news. If you have to play near the road, always stop and look carefully before crossing.

4

Stay out of other people's yards. A basic rule of the jungle is not to go into other animals' territory without permission. You'll get roared at if you do, and that's only the beginning of the trouble you can get into.

5

Wear a helmet if you're riding on any kind of fast-moving vehicle, be it bike, scooter, or skateboard. Nobody's head is made strong enough to handle hitting the sidewalk at high speeds. Even a tiger would need something over its ears before riding around on wheels.

6 Pay attention to what your body needs. Drink water, especially in warm weather. Bundle up when it's cold, and don't spend too long outside. You should always be able to feel all parts of your body. Take a lesson from a black bear—some cold days it is better just to sleep—for you, that would be inside.

7 Watch out for your brothers, sisters, and friends— whoever's with you—whether they're big or small. Be a good member of a wolf pack. Make sure everyone can keep up and is doing okay. Howling can be fun.

8 Take inside what you brought outside, toys, trash, whatever it is. Always leave the outside the way it was when you got there, in every way. Don't stomp on the flowers or tear leaves off trees, either. Even the smallest leaf has a job to do; your job is to make sure it gets a chance to do it.

9 Now that you've had a chance to get out and have a great time, make sure you can get back in! Take a key with you, so you can get back in your house. Being locked out of the cave always drives bats crazy . . . so don't go batty.

10 *Now GET OUT! Have fun! Enjoy the wild!*

Here's the key...

Which activities are right today?
Look for these clues on every page.

HOW HARD?

⌒ easy

⌒⌒ not so easy

⌒⌒⌒ difficult

HOW LONG?

☀ quarter of a day

☀ ☀ half a day

☀ ☀ ☀ whole day

HOW MANY PEOPLE?

Suggested number
for optimum fun:
1, 2, 3, 4, or
even more

TERRAIN

 pavement

grass

 anywhere

Got the Gear?

There's nothing like being prepared for a great day outside. Like to play ball? Put it where you can pick it up on your way out the door. The stuff you collect for GET OUT fun will depend on what's fun for you when you GET OUT. Here's a list of some of the things the kids featured in this book used.

Backpacks, baskets	Frisbee	**Popsicle sticks**
Bags, boxes	Garbage bags	**Poster board**
Balloons	Gardening tools, gloves	**Poster paints, brushes**
Balls of all sorts	Glue stick, stapler, scissors	**Ruler**
Bats, sticks	Hangers, clangers	**Snacks, drinks**
Bikes	Hole punch, ruler	**Soap, water**
Blankets, tarps	Jump rope, other rope	**Sponges, towels**
Buckets, cans	Lawn mower	**Straws, ribbon**
Building tools	Magnifying glass, binoculars	**String of all kinds**
Camera (instant)		**Table, chairs**
Cardboard tubes	Measuring cups, bowls	**Tape/CD player**
Clothes (old, comfortable)	Milk carton	**Tape of all kinds**
Clothesline	Nails, bolts, screws	**Watering can, hose**
Coins	Net, poles	**Wood scraps**
Colored chalk	Newspaper	**Ziplock bags, twisty ties**
Compass, stopwatch	Notebooks, paper	
Costumes, disguises	Pencils, pens	
Crayons, markers	Plants, seeds	
Cups, jars	Poles, trees	

TWO DRAGONS *wrestle each other to the ground, roaring and breathing fire. If only they had some new games to play, they say, they wouldn't be so cross. Show them how to toss a ball and throw a Frisbee, jump rope and bat balloons. This way, they will have games to play, and nobody will get burned. These GET OUT games will keep you and your dragon friends outside for hours having fun.*

Let the Games Begin

Let the Games Begin

Foot volley

If you think soccer is a kick and volleyball is a ball, try this fast-moving, high-stepping hybrid sport. You never know when this will be in the Olympics.

get ready

Net (volleyball net, rope and blanket, or string)

Poles (or trees, or sturdy chairs)

Ball (soccer ball, kick ball, beach ball, or balloon)

Coin

get set

How hard:

How long:

(easy to set up, but you can play all afternoon)

How many:

2 or more—the more, the merrier

Terrain:

get going!

1. Find a level spot at least 20 feet square (that's 20 feet on each side)—the larger, the better. Don't set up court close to any windows or fragile garden plants that might suffer from a missed kick.

2. Mark the boundaries of the court. It should be a rectangle, about twice as long as it is wide. Pick natural landmarks, like bushes and sidewalks, or mark the corners of the playing field with Frisbees, extra sweaters, or other things you find lying around.

3. Divide the court in half with the net. If you have a volleyball net, set up the poles and attach the net. Remember, the higher the net, the tougher it will be to kick the ball over. To make your own net, tie a piece of rope between two trees or a pair of lawn chairs. You can drape a blanket over the rope for extra "net" effect.

4. Pick teams and take a few practice "kicks." The idea is to get the ball over the net without using your hands or arms. It's just like soccer—you can use your feet, knees, head, butt, or any other part of the body but your hands and arms to move the ball. And it's like volleyball—each team has up to three "touches" to get the ball over the net without letting it hit the ground.

5. Game time: Flip a coin to see which team goes first. Each team gets to serve five times before switching, with all the players on one side taking turns serving. The server kicks the ball over to the other

side, and the other team must kick it back. The volley (or play) ends when one side is unable to return the ball to the other side, or when the ball goes out of bounds. If Team A kicks the ball and it lands on the same side of the net or goes out of bounds, Team B gets a point. If the kick lands inside the bounds on Team B's side, then Team A gets a point. The first team to get to 21 points wins the game.

Box ball

Box Ball is not a ball shaped like a box. It's not a box shaped like a ball, either. But it's more fun than a box full of balls.

get going!

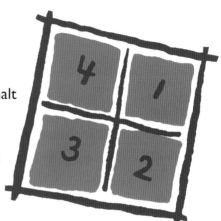

1. Find a piece of pavement in a playground or schoolyard or other asphalt for your game. Draw a chalk square that's 8 feet on each side. Then divide it into four small squares that measure 4 feet on a side. Label the squares 1, 2, 3, and 4, counting clockwise.

2. Box Ball (also known as Four Squares) is played a little like tennis. Each player stands inside one of the small squares. If there are more than four players, the extras should line up outside square 4. The player in square 1 serves by bouncing the ball in the square and then bonking it into one of the other squares. The player in that square then has to keep the ball in play by smacking it into any other square.

3. Hit the ball with an open hand or fist. No fair catching the ball and then throwing it back, or cradling the ball to get better control; that's called a "carry," and in cowboy days it would get you shot.

4. If the ball lands in your square and you don't hit it back, or if you hit the ball and it doesn't land in someone else's square, you're "out." You're also out if you get hit with the ball and it doesn't bounce off you into another square. Naturally, you're also out if someone calls you for a carry. But no shooting.

5. If there are only four players, the one who is out moves to square 4 and everyone else moves "up a number" toward number 1. If there are five of more players, the player who is out goes to the back of the line and the first person in line moves into square 4.

hot tips

- If you have fewer than four players, try playing "Two Squares." Just use half the court.

- Decide if you want to allow "spinners." That's when you hit the ball on its side and make it spin, so it bounces funny when it hits the ground.

Jump-rope games

Jumping! Spinning! Skipping! Running! Jumping rope is the most fun you can have while going nowhere fast.

get ready

1–2 jump ropes (cotton clothesline works great, too)

get set

How hard:

How long:

How many:
1–3 and on up

Terrain:

get going!

GOING SOLO

Fold the rope in half—when folded it should reach from the floor to your armpits. If it's too long, retie the knots at the handles or cut the clothesline to the right length.

The best way to learn the basics is to practice on your own. Hold the rope slack and step in front of it. Spin the rope over your head and hop over it with both feet just as it touches the ground. Work on keeping your rhythm smooth as you move the rope in this circular "forward" direction.

Some variations are spinning the rope forward and then backward, or skipping one foot at a time, or hopping up and down on just one foot at a time. See how fast you can go, and keep jumping as long as you can.

TEAM TIME

Two kids at a time take turns spinning the rope for the rest of the group to jump. (The rope should be at least 10 feet long.) Jumpers can run in one at a time or as a group. Try to learn trick moves, like running in, jumping a few times, and then running out while the rope whirls overhead. Bend down, touch the ground, and spin around. Make up chants to go along with the moves, or create routines to the tune of your favorite songs.

DOUBLE DUTCH

One rope not enough of a challenge for you? Try jumping two long ropes in sequence. Two twirlers, one on each side, hold a rope in each hand and spin them in opposite directions. The trick is to keep the rhythm going, rope 1, rope 2. That's a lot of rope to jump! Practiced twirlers can vary the rhythm from slow to fast and faster. Practiced jumpers just keep on jumping!

Frisbee golf

Put a new spin on two old sports. It's not your grandfather's golf and it's not your big brother's Frisbee game. This combo is twice as much fun, and you don't have to wear dorky golf clothes.

get ready

1 Frisbee per person

Pencil and paper

get set

How hard:

How long:

How many:

1 or more

Terrain:

get going!

1. Find a place to play with plenty of space. You can play in a big yard or a bigger park, or take your game "on the road" and set up a course that goes around the block and beyond.

2. The idea is to throw your Frisbee so it hits a goal; pick some targets with enough space around them for throwing. You can design a whole course ahead of time or decide the next goal as you play. (Traditional golf courses have 18 holes, but you can make as many as you want.)

3. Take turns throwing your Frisbee toward the goal. Everyone should stand in the same spot to start.

4. Once each player has thrown, walk together in the direction of the goal. As you reach each Frisbee, its owner gets to throw it again. (That way, nobody will get in the way and take a Frisbee to the noggin.)

	Carol	Mac	Jen
Big Tree	1	3	2
Bench	1	2	1
Little Tree	1	2	2
Trashcan	1	3	1
Total	4	10	6

5. Use the pencil and paper to keep track of how many throws it takes each person to hit the goal. To figure the final scores, add the totals for all the goals together. Lowest score wins.

hot tip

- Try playing blindfolded. Let your friends give you hints—left, right, higher, lower—to guide your throws and to help you find the Frisbee.

- Frisbee golf pros use baskets for goals, so try making one of your goals a basketball net or a big bucket.

now what?

Make colorful goals for Frisbee golfing at your next Papier-Mâché Party (see pages 40–41).

Balloon olympics

Invent your own lightweight decathlon for some heavy-duty fun. It's not as easy as it looks. Balloons can have minds of their own. And they're empty.

get ready

Balloons of various sizes

String for tying

Chalk

Bucket

get set

How hard:

How long:

How many:

2 or more

Terrain:

get going!

SHOOT OUT

Blow up and tie off six balloons, three for each player. Two players stand back to back, then walk three paces. On the count of 3, they turn around and start firing. The object is for each shooter to hit the other with the balloons before being hit. It's okay to duck and dodge and bend over to pick up extra balloons, but no fair taking your feet off the ground. Once hit, the player's out. The last one standing wins.

A group can play this game, too, so long as there's an even number of players. Just expand the number of balloons and the number of players standing back to back. Teams pace off and shoot at the other side. The team with the last member standing wins.

LONG JUMP

Mark a starting line on the ground with chalk. Blow up several big, round balloons. Place them on the ground, then run up to the starting line and jump over the balloons. Add another balloon after each successful jump. Each turn ends with a bang.

JET ARCHERY

Set a bucket on the ground and walk five paces away. Blow up a balloon, but don't tie it off. Try to shoot it into the bucket using its own jet power and listen to it whine through the air.

RELAY RACE

Divide the group into two teams. Mark a course. Team members stand at each end. At the starting line, set a balloon on the ground in front of each team. Ready, set, go! The first racers squat over their balloon, squeeze it between their legs (no hands!), and run, as best as they can, down to the other end. Then they pass the balloon with their legs to the next racer on their team. The first team whose racers get through the course wins. The results are hilarious.

Lead-and-follow games

If you're tired of your little brother saying, "Hey, you're not the boss of me," now's your chance to prove him wrong. The bad news is, he gets a turn to be your boss, too! Look at it this way: These timeless lead-and-follow games are a fun way to practice your leadership potential.

get ready

Comfortable clothes

get set

How hard:

How long:

How many:
3 or more

Terrain:

get going!

FOLLOW THE LEADER

Pick a leader. Follow her. Wherever she goes. However she gets there. Up a tree, under a ladder, or around and around and around in tiny circles until you all get so dizzy you can't tell which way is up. Skipping, or running, or crawling like a crab. The game ends when you finally say, "Enough!"

Note: Do not do anything that feels unsafe or un-fun to you. If your leader is giving orders that you don't feel right following, it may be time for a revolution. But as long as she can avoid any rebellions, the leader gets to decide how long the game goes on and who will be in charge next.

MOTHER, MAY I?

Mothers can be tricky. Even when you think you're doing what you're supposed to, it's sometimes better to double-check. In this game, the person who is Mother gives the other players instructions, one at a time. If Mother says, "Take ten baby steps," you must first ask, "Mother, may I?" and wait for the answer. He can either say, "Yes, you may" or "No, you may not." Mothers get to do whatever they want to. If you aren't polite and forget to ask permission before you take your baby steps, Mother will send you back to the starting point. When Mother gets tired of giving the orders, he can pick the next Mother.

now what?

Play Follow the Leader on bikes, (see Eat and Ride, pages 38–39), or on hikes, or on the way to your Picnic (see pages 34–35).

RED LIGHT, GREEN LIGHT

Lesson number one at traffic school is: A red light means Stop and a green light means Go. Find a good-sized piece of open territory, like a backyard or an empty stretch of playground. Choose one side for the starting line. Pick a player to be Traffic Cop, and send him across the field. The rest of the group lines up at the starting line and gets ready to go. The Cop turns his back and shouts "Green light," and everyone starts moving toward the Cop. After a few seconds, the Cop yells "Red light" and turns around to face the group. If he sees any players who are still moving, he sends them back to the starting line. The first person to tag the Cop wins and gets to do the job next time. You have to move fast enough to get there first, but not so fast that you can't stop in time.

Lead-and-follow games, too!

Okay, now it's time for someone else to lead and everyone else to follow. Who's next?

get ready

Comfortable clothes

get set

How hard:

How long:

How many:

3 or more

Terrain:

get going!

SIMON SAYS

Pick someone to be Simon. Simon stands in front, and the rest of the group lines up facing her. Simon gives instructions. If she says, "Simon says, touch your toes," you must follow the order. If she just says, "Touch your nose," do not follow the order! If you don't do a "Simon says" command, or if you do follow a Simon-less order, you're out. Simon should try to find ways to trick the other players, like going fast, and everyone else should pay careful attention to keep from being tricked. The last player standing gets to become Simon in the next game.

H-O-R-S-E

Play this game while shooting hoops, doing gymnastics, or riding a skateboard. Decide who goes first. That person names a shot to shoot or a trick to try, and then he tries to do it. If he doesn't make it, the next player chooses a trick. If she's successful, everyone else has to try the same trick. Every time players miss, they get a letter: first H, then O, R, S, and E. Once they can spell out "horse," they're out.

Here are few variations:

* For a shorter game, spell out C-A-T.
* For a longer game, spell T-Y-R-A-N-N-O-S-A-U-R-U-S.
* Another way to start the game is for the first player to keep going until she messes up. After that, the other players get to try.
* Each mimicking player only gets one turn at a time; that way, each missed play only counts for one letter.

hot tip

Let the first person to be It pick the game. Whoever wins gets to be
It and decide what to play next.

THE ANIMAL KINGDOM

has lots of parties and events. Crows gather over everything from food to sunsets. Lionesses hunt together. Male cranes do an amazing song and dance to impress their females. Be lions by snacking and packing. Be scavenger hunters and picnic makers. GET OUT your dancing shoes, and make merry like the cranes and crows. There are many eventful ways for you and your beast friends to have fun together.

Eventful Events

Eventful Events

Pack a picnic

Climb every mountain. Ford every stream. Carry every backpack. Grab every food you're allowed to eat. Go somewhere natural and beautiful. Give yourself a tummyache in the great outdoors.

get ready

Food and drinks

Napkins and plastic bags

Blanket

Backpack or picnic basket

Trail snacks

get set

How hard:

How long:

(easy to get ready, stay all day)

How many:

1 or more

Terrain:

get going!

1. Choose your picnic spot. All the best picnic sites have a view of some kind. People-watching in a crowded park. Bird-watching in the woods. Car-watching from the sidewalk. But don't forget your front steps or backyard—they could perfect places for outside dining!

2. Keep your meal simple. Instead of toting cups, bring a bottle that you can drink from. Fix food that you can eat with your fingers. Sandwiches and cold chicken legs are classic picnic food, so there's no need to pack forks and knives. Make sure you bring plenty of napkins for cleaning up for the return trip, and bring a plastic bag for all of your trash. If you don't find garbage and recycling containers at your picnic site, you'll have to pack out whatever you packed in.

If people-watching is on the agenda for your picnic, bring a notebook and practice your spying (see pages 56–57). If your destination is somewhere where the wildlife isn't human, bring a Nature Scrapbook (pages 72–73) and a pencil to record your observations, or collect mementos for making a wind chime (pages 90–91) or handmade paper (pages 78–79).

Getting there can be half the fun. Why not play a game of Follow the Leader (page 26) or Frisbee Golf (pages 22–23) on your way to lunch?

3. Throw your feast into a backpack or picnic basket, along with a blanket to sit on, and hit the trail. All this travel is bound to work up an appetite, so make sure you bring snacks to eat along the way. GORP (Good Old Raisins and Peanuts, plus chocolate chips) is a favorite snack for back-packers, and is easy to eat as you go.

4. Once you arrive at your destination, unpack the blanket, stretch out, and dig in.

Scavenger hunt

Finders, keepers. Finders, keepers. Finders, keepers. Finders, keepers. Finders, keepers. Finders, keepers. Got it? Good.

get ready

Notepaper and pen

Bag or box to store treasures in

Instant camera (optional)

Unusual items to hide

get set

How hard:

How long:

How many:
2 or more

Terrain:

get going!

1. Decide on the boundaries for your hunt. It can be limited to your backyard or extend to your whole town. Be realistic and make it safe.

2. Set a time limit. You can play this game in less than an hour, or you can take all summer long. Don't forget, you can play it again and again.

3. Figure out who the competition is. Each player can be his or her own hunter. But it's also fun to hunt in teams.

4. Decide on categories for the treasures and write them down. Some things to find may be information that you can write down (or photograph with an instant camera). Perhaps you'll make a map of the oldest buildings in town, or the tallest ones. Maybe you'll have to list all the houses with trees in their front yard. Other items may be things to bring home, like a worm or a toad. Just don't let the toad eat the worm. See who can bring back the most returnable deposit bottles or the blackest rock.

5. Hide some treasures of your own. Each player or team can hide something somewhere within the boundaries. Show all the players what you're hiding, and make sure they'll know it when they see it. Don't make your treasure so small that no one can find it, or else you might lose it yourself. And don't hide something so common that anyone can find something just like it.

now what?

Make odd shapes for hiding out of papier-mâché (see pages 40–41), or use a scavenger hunt to add to your insect and worm collections (see pages 68–69).

6. Set a place to meet when time is up or when everyone is finished. Figure out how you'll decide who won in different categories. Appoint a judge? Decide as a group? Give prizes for the fastest, the biggest, the smallest, and the funniest collections of treasures.

hot tip

You can have different types of hunts. Consider an "opposite" hunt, where you have to find opposite objects, such as big and small things; a "red" hunt, where you have to find only red things; and so on. Make up your own.

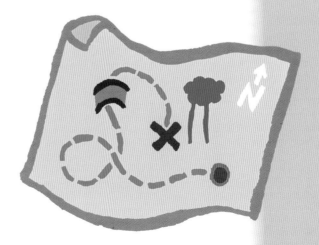

Eat and ride

They say it's not polite to eat and run. So don't do it. Eat and ride on bikes instead. You and your friends will be in and out of more kitchens than a refrigerator repairman.

get ready

Bikes

Snacks

get set

How hard:

How long:

How many:
2 or more

Terrain:

get going!

1. Pick a meeting spot and get a bunch of friends together.

2. Everyone gets to take turns deciding where to go and what snack to eat next. This person shall be known as Snackmaster. Decide who gets to be the first Snackmaster. Also agree ahead of time if you want to spend money or just raid each other's refrigerators. Maybe Snackmaster will call for a trip to her house for hot fudge sundaes, to your house for your Dad's famous cookies that he just happened to bake last night, to the ballpark for hot dogs, or to the beach for fried clams.

3. No fair making any one of the snackers or anyone's parents do all the hard work—a Snackmaster who wants fresh-picked strawberries will have to help with the picking.

4. Don't make a big pig of yourself. The idea is to sample a little bit of lots of different snacks, not to eat until you explode. Share those sundaes and split those bananas, so you can all go the distance. And don't spend too much money, either.

5. Once you've all had your fill at the first stop, it's time to head back out on the trail of treats: Pick the next Snackmaster and hit the road. The last stop can be at the hospital to get your stomach pumped!

now what?

In between snacks is a perfect time to play **Lead-and-Follow Games** (see pages 26–27). Snackmaster gets to be It first, of course.

Are you keeping a secret **Spy Journal** with a study of your friends' behavior (see pages 56–57)? Make sure to take good notes about their feeding habits.

hot tip

One good way to pick the Snackmaster is by voting: Everyone suggests a next stop on the snack train, and the whole crew votes. Whoever gets the most votes is in charge.

Papier-mâché party

Papier-mâché is possibly the world's messiest art form. It's made by mixing torn strips of paper with glue. Papier-mâché means "chewed paper" in French.

get ready

Tarp or other work-area cover

Smocks or old T-shirts

Sculpture skeletons (balloons, cardboard tubes, aluminum foil)

Scissors

Old newspapers, magazines, paper towels, and other throwaway paper

Buckets, bowls, or pans

Flour and water for glue

Measuring cups (dry and wet)

Poster paint (tempera) and markers

get set

How hard:

How long:

How many:

2 or more

Terrain:

get going!

1. Find a level surface to work on, like a picnic table, driveway, or patio. Cover the work surface completely with a plastic tarp, drop cloth, or newspaper. You can also put down giant-sized garbage bags or an old sheet that your folks set aside for rags. Messes make moms and dads miserable.

2. Decide what kind of sculpture you want to make and collect material for making a mold for it. For example, to make a giant head, blow up a balloon. Use aluminum foil to shape eyebrows and an inch or two of cardboard tubing to make eyes that pop out. Another option is to make the head a simpler, smaller shape, and paint on the eyes and ears and other features. Set the materials aside (a balloon stores nicely in a bowl) while you prepare the paper and glue.

3. Start preparing your paper-and-glue medium by ripping some paper into strips about 1 inch wide and 6 inches long. Newspaper works well for building the sculpture, but if you are planning to apply paint, you'll need several layers to cover the printer's ink. That's why tissue paper and paper towels work better for the outside layers. For each balloon or similar-sized skeleton, you will need about four sheets of paper.

now what?

Not sure what to make? How about a papier-mâché decoration for your Barnless Barn Dance (see pages 46–47), a goal for your Frisbee Golf course (see pages 22–23), or a special mascot for your Fortified Fort (see pages 66–67)?

4. Find a container large enough for making the glue and dipping the strips into. Mix 3 cups of water with 2 cups of flour, and make more glue as you need it.

5. Before you get your hands into this messy stuff, put on a smock or old T-shirt to protect your clothes from the gooey glop. Dip a strip of paper into the glue. Scrape off the excess glop with your fingers, and smooth the strip onto your skeleton. If you are using foil or cardboard to fashion shapes, stick them onto the balloon using a gluey strip of paper.

6. Cover the entire surface of your skeleton with a layer of paper. (If you want to remove the balloon from inside the head, leave a 2-inch hole at the bottom to pull the popped balloon out of.) Continue to add more layers for strength. If you are planning to paint your work of art, make the top layer or two with plain white paper (see step 3).

7. Let the papier-mâché dry overnight before painting it. Voilà, your pièce de résistance (there, your showpiece)!

Blue-ribbon pet show

Show off your favorite furry, feathered, slimy, or scaly friends for everyone to see.

get ready

Pets

Judges' notebooks and pens or pencils

Blue ribbons and pet treats

get set

How hard:

How long:

How many:
3 or more

Terrain:

get going!

1. Find a good spot for the pet show. If you are inviting different kinds of animals, either schedule cats and dogs (and snakes and gerbils) for different times, or make sure there is plenty of room to keep them separated. You want a show, not a scramble. There should be enough space for all the animals, with their owners in tow, to sit or stand and be viewed for their looks, plus an area for tricks and obedience competitions.

2. Let people know about the event ahead of time, so you can get as many pets and spectators as possible to participate. If you don't have many participants, hold events one at a time to stretch it out.

3. Decide what categories you want to have in the competition. The more categories you have, the more winners there can be. Make rules for the categories, and tell the competitors' owners how their loved ones will be judged. Try ranking the animals from 1 to 10, or give them letter grades. (Will the prettiest iguana get an A+?) Besides judging looks and obedience, have contests for the funniest trick, the highest jump, and the pet that looks the most like its owner.

4. Choose judges for the contests who you are sure will be fair. You might want to have a cat owner judge the dogs to avoid favoritism. Make sure the judges take notes and keep score.

5. To pick the best-looking animals, try to have them sit still so the judges can see them up close, and then have them scamper around the arena, so everyone can see them in action. (If turtles are in the

show, make sure the arena is not too big, or this could take a long time.) Owners should say a few words about what they like best about their pets.

6. For the obedience section, have the dog owners call their pets, then tell them to sit and stay. (Cats that obey any commands at all automatically win a prize!) Set up an obstacle course, have a fetching contest, and allow some freestyle tricks where anything goes.

7. After the scores are tallied, have an awards ceremony. Give each owner whose pet wins a prize a blue ribbon, and give each winning pet a treat, such as a doggie bone, or catnip, or fish food for the fastest swimmer. (P.S.: Dogs hate fish food, and vice versa.)

hot tip

If competition isn't your game, try organizing a pet parade.

Talent extravaganza

Everybody loves to sing in the shower and dance in the dark, although it's dangerous to try them together. But if you want to make the big time—or just have big-time fun—you've got to turn off the water and turn on the lights, and take your talent out in the open.

get ready

Seats for the audience

Portable tape or CD player for background music

Each performer brings costumes and equipment

get set

How hard:

How long:

How many:
2 or more

Terrain:

get going!

1. Step right up! Find a good spot for the performances to take place. There should be space up front for the talent to strut their stuff, and plenty of room for the crowd to sit comfortably while watching the spectacle. If you don't have enough lawn chairs for all the guests you expect, ask them to bring their own. Or spread blankets or towels on the ground for them to sit on.

2. Organize your performers. If you want to do a Really Big Show, give participants plenty of time, so that everyone who wants to be in the show can plan ahead. Try to get a good mix of acts: Do you know anyone who juggles, sings, or dances? How about a master whistler or an expert at making silly faces?

3. All of the performers should invite their friends and family. If you want a Really Big Crowd, put up posters and sidewalk chalk signs, so the whole neighborhood knows when and where the event will take place. You could also choose to take your show someplace where crowds form on their own, like a park or a safe public place.

4. Decide what order the performers should go on, and make sure everyone knows when their turn is, so the show will keep moving smoothly. Choose an announcer to introduce the acts. (It should be someone with a Really Big Mouth.) If you have time, do a full rehearsal to guarantee that everything will run smoothly.

5. If the tape/CD player (for background music) is running on batteries, make sure the batteries are fresh.

6. Just before showtime, tell everyone to "break a leg." That's show-biz slang for "good luck!" So don't really break a leg, okay?

7. Break a leg!

8. But not really!

Barnless barnyard dance

Music is just as good in the city! You can have a barnyard without a barn, square dance without a square, and listen to bluegrass on a gray sidewalk.

get ready

Paper, cardboard tubes

Markers, paint, crayons

Tape

Portable tape/CD player and down-home country music

"Country" costumes

get set

How hard:

How long:

How many:
2 or more

Terrain:

get going!

1. Find a good location for your "barnyard." There should be plenty of room for dancing, playing games, and serving refreshments.

2. Invite your friends over for a good time, and tell them to dress like farmers—or like farm animals, if they happen to look good as a pig or a goat.

3. Decorate your barnyard so it looks (sort of) like the real thing: Make pitchforks out of construction paper and cardboard tubes, draw chickens and cows, and fill the horses' stable with strips of newspaper for straw.

4. Fellas, wear your best overalls, plaid shirts, and straw hats. Gals, wear long skirts, plaid blouses, and straw hats. You can make straw hats out of yellow construction paper; make a few extra for your guests.

5. Serve refreshments with a barnyard theme: Set out fresh pie, cold milk, and a bowl of broken tortilla chips with a sign that says "chicken feed."

6. Play your tape or CD collection of country music, folk songs, and blue-grass tunes, and "do-si-do your partners to and fro," square-dance style.

7. Have a contest to see who can do the best animal impersonation. Who can walk like a chicken? Can anyone make a sound like a real pig? A rooster? A sheep? You can even have a cow!

 hot tip

Think of other kinds of theme parties you can have outside. How about a jungle boogie? Or, next time it's stormy, try a Singin'-in-the-Rain Sing-along.

now what?

Try making barnyard animals at your next Papier-Mâché Party (see pages 40–41).

THE SIDEWALK *is where the action is. In the concrete jungle, there is always something happening—other kids out for some fun, people bringing home groceries and coming home from work. The sidewalk is the best place to draw pictures with chalk and display your artwork to passersby. The game of broom ball would be lost without one. So, GET OUT in the neighborhood and become part of the sidewalk beat.*

The Sidewalk Beat

The Sidewalk Beat

Sidewalk chalk

Got something to say that you want the whole world to know? Got something to show that you think everyone should see? Grab your chalk and take it to the streets. Hint: Not recommended on rainy days.

get ready

Colored chalk

get set

How hard:

How long:

How many:
1 or more

Terrain:

get going!

1. Decide what you want to do with your chalk. You can draw a picture or write a poem. You can just sit on your front stoop and doodle whatever comes to mind. Or perhaps you'll plan a complicated treasure hunt, writing clues in chalk that lead people from spot to spot all over town.

2. Find a good place for your project. The beauty of sidewalk art is that you can do it anywhere there's cement. If you want to be an artist and make one big drawing, the sidewalk in front of your house is fabulous. If you want to be a cartoonist, make every cement square or rectangle in your patio a frame in a cartoon. If you want to share a message with passersby, it can be a serious one, like "Don't litter," or a silly one, like telling riddles and knock-knock jokes up and down your block. (Here's a good one: Q: What did one wall say to the other wall? A: Meet you at the corner.) If you want to be a storyteller, write a story one sentence at a time that starts at your house and ends across town. Add a new line every day and the story will never end.

3. Try to make your drawing big and bright so people will notice it as they walk by (unless you are writing a secret message that you want to keep hidden from everyone except your best friend).

4. Be careful not to smudge the chalk as you draw and write. But if it does get wrecked, clean off the sidewalk with some water and start again.

now what?

Sidewalk chalk is a great way to **advertise your business** (see pages 112–125) or **special event** (pages 42–47). You can also use chalk to draw the strike zone and bases in a **Broom Ball** game (see pages 60–61) or the court for a game of **Box Ball** (see pages 18–19). And what about using sidewalk chalk in your next **Scavenger Hunt** (pages 36–37)?

Texture rubbings

Life's rough. Use paper and crayon to capture the cracks, crevices, bumps, and blisters of the rough, rough world under your feet and all around you. You'll rub the world the right way.

get ready

Paper

Masking tape or weights (optional)

Crayons or chalk

get set

How hard:

How long:

How many:
1 or more

Terrain:

get going!

1. Find something with an interesting texture. It could be a shattered stretch of sidewalk, the raspy bumps of a brick wall, the lettering on a metal manhole cover or cable TV access box, or the ridges of a tree's rough bark.

SAFETY NOTE: Don't crouch down in the middle of the sidewalk behind a hedge or around a corner, where someone can't see you and might trip on you. Or worse, don't go in the middle of the street, where you could get flattened by a car and become an interesting texture yourself.

2. Lay your paper down over the targeted texture. Put stones or other heavy objects around the edges of your paper, or tape down the corners—whatever method works to keep the paper from moving— unless you want the image to be jumbled and jumpy, which can be quite awesome, too.

3. Pick the rubbing material. Peel the paper off a crayon so you can rub with the whole side. This is a great way to use broken crayons or crayons that have worn down so short that they're hard to draw with. Another medium is colored chalk (just keep blowing away the chalk dust).

4. Rub the rubbing medium up and down the paper. If you rub too hard, you will color in the whole paper and wipe out all of the texture. You might also rip your paper. If you don't rub hard enough, the lines and bumps of the texture will be too faint to see. Good luck.

5. Try layering different textures on the same piece of paper. Just pick your paper up, find a new texture to rub, lay your paper down, secure it, and go again. Use the same crayon or try a different color. You're bound to end up with "environmental art" at its finest!

 ### hot tip

Try making a "scratching" using colored pencils, preferably with soft, wide lead.

Spy Journal

To become a spy journalist, all you need are a keen sense of curiosity and your own powers of observation. Binoculars are optional. Watch people to see what they do and what they say. Then write about them or draw their picture. Don't let them catch you watching!

get ready

Notebook and pen or pencil

Sunglasses, reading material, binoculars (optional)

Stopwatch, tape recorder, camera (optional)

get set

How hard:

How long:

How many:

I or more

Terrain:

get going!

1. Pick a group of people to watch—the grown-ups who walk to and from work every day, kids on the block, or even your own friends and family.

2. Start watching your subjects carefully. Think about every little thing they do as if you were a total outsider—like an alien from outer space or an exchange student from a foreign land. Write down the details of every observation and make sketches of what you see. What kind of clothes do they wear? How do they walk, fast or slow? What kinds of greetings do they use? Do they touch each other when they meet, hugging or shaking hands? How close do they stand to one another when they talk? What kind of food do they eat? Do they play any games? What kinds of tools do they use? Do they seem happy or sad, friendly or reserved? Remember, act like you've never seen them before.

3. Spies usually don't like to be watched while they're watching. Wear sunglasses, read a newspaper, or play a game, so people don't realize you are looking at them. You can observe them from a distance using binoculars—as long as you don't "invade anyone's privacy," which means watching them where they never expect to be seen by anyone

else. No peeking into windows or backyards; that's not spying, it's snooping. On the other hand, many secret agents work out in the open, with no tricks or disguises, and find that they blend right into the scenery.

4. Decide if you want to take notes as you observe, or wait until later to do your writing and sketching. You may want to use a stopwatch, a tape recorder, or a camera to record other kinds of data, such as the amount of time it takes your subjects to say good-bye, a recording of the songs they sing, or a photo of some of their typical behaviors.

5. Share your research with your friends. Perhaps they'll want to observe with you and add to what you have discovered.

Art show

Don't just stick your favorite masterpieces on the refrigerator—share them with the world at your own open-air art gallery.

get ready

Crayons, pen, and paper, or chalk

Artworks

Tools and supplies for displaying

Labels

Guest book and pen

Refreshments

get set

How hard:

How long:

How many:

I or more

Terrain:

get going!

1. Find a good spot for your outdoor gallery, with enough room to hang all the art you want to show.

2. Decide how to tell people about the show. Are there enough people just passing by, or do you need to put up signs and announcements? To advertise, make handwritten or photo-copied flyers, or write sidewalk signs with chalk. Pick a time for your show when people will be in the area. If you live near a subway or bus stop, plan your show for the afternoon rush hour when commuters are headed home, or set up your display in a park on a sunny weekend.

3. Hang your artwork. Tape pictures to a wall or garage door, use pushpins or thumbtacks to hang them from trees with thick bark, or tie rope between two poles or trees and hang them with clothespins or large paperclips. If you're displaying pottery, masks, or jewelry, you may want something to put them on, like tables or boxes with cloth or paper coverings. If you decide to put them on the ground with no covering, be very careful not to break them.

4. Does your art have titles? Attach a tag with information like the name of the piece, the date when you made it, and the medium you used to create it, like watercolors, magic markers, or papier-mâché.

now what?

Try to plan your show so that it coincides with other big events. Is a neighborhood Yard Sale coming up (see pages 124–125)?

Why not show off the creations you made at your Papier-Mâché Party (see pages 40–41) with a gala exhibition?

Do any of your friends have a Lemonade Stand (see pages 116–117)? Maybe you could ask them to provide refreshments for your art show.

5. Serve refreshments. Nothing makes works of art look prettier than a tasty snack and a delicious beverage.

6. Mingle. Talk with your visitors about your art. Ask them to sign your guest book and write down their thoughts about your art show. They may have interesting ideas that will inspire your next creative project.

hot tip

Are your friends all artists, too? Why not ask them if you can organize a show of all their works? Pick your favorite pictures and other types of art, and put on a group show. The more, the merrier.

Batter-up broom ball

Put a new twist on an old tradition. In the 1950s, players from the New York Yankees used to play an inning or two in neighborhood stickball matches, using any stick they could find. Give a new function to the household sweeping tool—grab a broom and head out for a game of broom ball.

get ready

Chalk

Ball (a racquetball, tennis ball, or squash ball is good)

Bat (a broomstick, mop handle, or anything you can swing)

get set

How hard:

How long:

How many:

2 or more

Terrain:

get going!

1. Pick a playing area. With just a few players, you can play against a stoop or a wall, with the wall "playing" as catcher. With more players, you can play on pavement in a schoolyard or playground.

SAFETY NOTE: Do not play in the street at all, and do not play on a sidewalk that is close to a street where there is traffic.

2. Decide on the boundaries and the bases. Mark the distance a ball needs to be hit to count as a single, a double, a triple, or a home run. Use natural features for bases, like lampposts, tree stumps, or park benches, or mark them on the ground with chalk. If you're playing against a wall, draw a box for the strike zone on the wall. (It should be between the shoulders and the knees of most of the kids, and about 18 inches wide.) And nowhere near windows.

3. Choose teams and decide who gets to pitch first. The pitcher throws the ball toward the batter. It has to bounce once before it passes the batter.

4. Try to hit the pitch as far as you can. If you get a hit, check how far it went to see what kind of hit it was. If there is a player "on second base" and the next batter hits a double, the first player scores,

because he gets to go two bases, and that's home plate. A single plus a triple equals one run and one player on third, and so on.

5. If you swing and miss, hit the ball foul, or let the ball hit the strike zone, it is a strike. Three strikes and you're out. If you hit the ball and the other team catches it, you're out. When the hitting team gets three outs, it's their turn to pitch.

6. Decide how long you want to play, and make sure each team gets a fair chance to bat before the game ends.

7. Change the rules to fit your neighborhood. You can run bases, just like regular baseball, if you have a good "field" to play on. If you're short on players, batters can "pitch" to themselves. Part of the fun of broom ball is making the rules fit your game.

HERE IS NATURE *from the ground up, from your fingers in the dirt looking for bugs to watching seeds grow into plants. Lie on your belly and feel the ground underneath you. Pull up grass to make paper with. **GET OUT** in your garden, go inside your fort, and let nature have its way. You will get dirt under your fingernails, leaves in your hair, and animal dreams in your head, as you explore the nitty-gritty of the world around you.*

Better Nature

Better Nature

Fortified fort

Be it ever so humble, there's no place like your very own, homemade, top-secret, what's the password, members-only fort.

get ready

Plastic tarp and pieces of wood

Rope, clothespins

Tools (yardstick or measuring tape, hammer, screwdriver, saw)

Nails or screws

Cardboard, paint, and paintbrush

get set

How hard:

How long:

How many:

1 or more

Terrain:

get going!

1. Find a spot to build your fort. It should be someplace where you can go if you feel like "lying low." How about under the picnic table or the back porch? Among the trees in the backyard? Check with an adult to make sure that you're building your fort somewhere safe, and make sure they know where you are.

2. Collect building materials like wood scraps and a plastic tarp to build the walls of the fort.

3. Plan an entrance (and maybe a secret exit) and windows, so you can peer out to see if anyone is spying on your secret hideout.

4. Think about what your skills are when you are deciding what features you want to build into your fort. Don't try to use tools you don't know how to handle, and don't build high in a tree without some help from a grown-up who knows about these things.

5. Build your fort. You can make a temporary enclosure by just leaning wood against a wall or draping a tarp over rope and securing it with clothespins. You can build a more permanent one with wood and nails or screws, but definitely get permission.

   SAFETY NOTE: If you will be hammering or using old wood that can cause splinters, put gloves on to protect your hands. And make sure an adult is nearby to help with any problems that may occur!

6. Paint a sign for your fort. Give the building a name and put out a welcome sign. Maybe instead you'll want to hang a "No big brothers allowed" sign to keep the "riff-raff" out of your special spot.

now what?

Got any nuts and bolts left over from building your fort? Make a **Jingly Wind Chime** (see pages 90–91), so you'll know if stormy weather is heading toward your hideout.

hot tips

- If you use nails and screws, drive them all the way into the wood, and don't let points stick out the other end.

- Measure each piece of wood twice with a yardstick or measuring tape before you saw it. That way, you'll avoid making mistakes that you can't fix.

Creepy crawly collecting

There's a whole world of creatures who creep, crawl, leap, wriggle, walk, and stalk right under your nose. Or at least under your feet, if you want to keep your nose especially clean.

get ready

Notebook and pen

Magnifying glass

Field guide

Trowel

Clear jar with lid

get set

How hard:

How long:

How many:

1 or more

Terrain:

get going!

1. Invertebrates are animals without a backbone, like insects, arachnids, and worms, to name just a few kinds. They live just about anywhere you can imagine, but there are a few good places to look: near water, under rocks, in dirt, and especially where things are rotting, like the bottom of a layer of leaves in a wood. Pick one of these places—a habitat—to explore at a time. Later, you can compare your findings from different habitats.

2. Once you pick a spot for your search, take a few moments to look over the whole scene. Are any big bugs flying around or floating on the surface of a puddle? What kinds of plants grow nearby? Is the soil moist or dry? Are there any odd smells? Use all five senses to experience your surroundings. Write down your observations in a notebook.

3. Take a closer look, and start searching for critters. Get right down to their level. Pick 1 square inch of soil and stare at it to see if there are any tiny insects moving around that you missed before. Take out your magnifying glass and move in even closer.

4. What do you see? Try to identify as many creatures as you can, using your field guide. Watch for a while and see how the creatures behave. What does a spider do while it waits for a fly? How do the ants move through the area? What do different bugs do when they meet each other? What do they seem to be eating?

now what?

**Make sketches of
your favorite worms
and flies for your
Nature Scrapbook
(see pages 72–73).**

5. Use a trowel to dig a little deeper, under rocks or into a loose layer
of topsoil, and you will find a whole new cast of characters. Be very
careful when you're scooping up dirt not to harm the tiny creatures
or the greenery.

6. If you want to take a closer look at your mini-zoo, put your subjects in a
clear jar. Make plenty of air holes in the top, and fill the bottom of the jar
with dirt and leaves from the habitat where you picked up your specimens,
so they feel at home. Keep them just long enough to get to know them,
and then set them free. These little creatures do all kinds of important
work, like breaking down dead plants
to make new soil, eating other bugs,
and feeding fish and birds. So
they're needed back where they
came from.

Leaf art

Who says great works of art don't grow on trees?
You can use leaves to paint, print, and draw
artworks that are beautiful, naturally.

get ready

Newspaper

Leaves (from trees, plants, grass)

Markers and crayons

Bowls and plates

Paints and brushes

Construction paper and glue stick

get set

How hard:

How long:

How many:
1 or more

Terrain:

get going!

1. Collect a variety of leaves with different shapes, textures, and colors. Look for interesting patterns of veins, lobes, and edges. If it is autumn, you might find many different colors of leaves in your corner of the world.

2. Find a flat, level place to spread out and work, like a sidewalk, picnic table, or patio floor. Spread newspaper out to protect the surface from paint spills. Organize your supplies. Put your collection of leaves on one side, and arrange paints, brushes, and markers where you can reach them.

3. Hold a leaf down on a sheet of construction or other heavy paper and gently trace its edges with a crayon or marker.

4. If you want to use paint, spread some colors in the bowls and plates. Dip a leaf to cover it with paint, then press it down on the paper so that the leaf pattern becomes imprinted onto it. Repeat this procedure with the same or different leaves to make an interesting pattern. Try overlapping colors and patterns. You can also trace leaf shapes, then paint in or color them.

5. Pick some especially lovely leaves and glue-stick them to the picture.

now what?

Paste your favorite leaf-art projects in your Nature Scrapbook (see pages 72–73), or use the painted leaves in your handmade Nature Paper (see pages 78–79), or display your leaf rubbings at your next Art Show (see pages 58–59).

hot tip

You may want to paint and draw with colors that are not present in your leaves, like blue or neon pink. Also consider adding similar shades of color to enhance the natural colors, such as greens, browns, and oranges in autumn.

Nature scrapbook

Turn over a new leaf every day! Make a special book to write down your observations about the great outdoors. It's your own place to keep souvenirs of your adventures and discoveries.

get ready

Notebook, pens, and pencils

Magnifying glass

Ruler

Cellophane tape

Ziplock plastic bags

Paints, markers, colored pencils

Glue stick

get set

How hard:

How long:

How many:

I or more

Terrain:

get going!

1. Decide what kind of scrapbook you want. It can be an inexpensive, rough-and-ready, spiral-bound notebook to take with you whenever and wherever you do exploring, or it can be a beautiful keepsake book that you keep all your special treasures in.

2. Start filling your book. Include scientific data that you observe, as well as poems, sketches, and paintings. Whenever you're out exploring, take paper and pens and pencils with you, so you can make notes and sketches in the field. With a magnifying glass, you'll be able to study tiny creatures too small to see with the naked eye. A ruler lets you measure the size of the bugs and seeds and flowers that you find. You can even bring samples back, either taped right into your book or carried in a plastic bag.

3. If you want to indulge your artistic side, take paints, markers, and other art supplies into the field with you, too. You might want to paint right in your book, or paste your favorite paintings in later. (Let paintings dry before closing the book.)

4. Spend a few minutes sitting in your favorite natural spots, just writing down everything you see, hear, smell, and feel.

5. Get as full a sense of nature as you can by combining objective observations, like the size of a giant mushroom, with your own feelings and impressions, like a poem about the way a dragonfly hovers over a pond.

A notebook is a great place to keep track of your other nature projects. Record rainfall measurements from your Engaging Rain Gauge (see pages 84–85) and list the kinds of birds that come to your Bird Feeder (see pages 92–93). Describe the growth of your Grocery Garden (see pages 76–77) and collect your favorite leaves and grass for Leaf Art and Nature Paper (see pages 70–71 and 72–73).

Make your own dirt

Some kids make everything dirty, but other kids actually make dirt. Find out soil's dirty secret: It's alive! Plus, making dirt is good, clean fun.

get ready

Chopping knife

Kitchen scraps

Newspaper

2 plastic Ziplock bags

Garden soil

Alfalfa pellets or green grass

Water

Magic marker

Bucket or box with lid

get set

How hard:

How long:

How many:

1 or more

Terrain:

get going!

1. Chop up two or three handfuls of organic matter: potato peels, banana skins, newspaper, dead leaves. Do not use meat scraps or animal products like milk, butter, or cheese, and do not use cooked food. The smaller the bits, the faster your garbage will become dirt.

2. Put half of the chopped material in each plastic bag. Add ¹/₂ cup of garden soil and about a tablespoon of alfalfa pellets—sold at pet stores as rabbit food—or a handful of green grass. Sprinkle a few spoonfuls of water on top. Close the bags and shake them up to mix the ingredients well.

3. Label the bags with a marker. On the first bag, write "Open" and on the second one write "Closed."

4. Set the bags inside a bucket or box with a lid, and put it where it won't be bothered. In hot weather, keep the container out of the sun; in cold weather, don't let your bags freeze.

5. Every day, mix up the contents of the bags and look for signs that things are starting to decompose. The bag that's labeled "Closed" should remain sealed. Unseal the "Open" bag every other day to air it out; seal it on Monday, then leave it open on Tuesday, seal it again on Wednesday, and so on. If it starts to dry out, sprinkle a few more spoonfuls of water inside.

6. Once a week, open each bag to examine the contents. Check for signs of life. Look for little insects scurrying around or mold growing in fuzzy patches. Smell each bag and notice any differences. Don't leave the "Closed" bag unsealed for long, and squeeze out as much air as you can.

7. Watch and smell the changes for six weeks. Different types of creatures thrive in the two distinct environments you have created. Both are decomposing the waste material you fed them, but one is a whole lot stinkier than the other one is.

now what?

You can use the dirt you made as fertilizer for your Grocery Garden (see pages 76–77).

Grow a grocery garden

Instead of swallowing those watermelon seeds, or spitting them at your brother or sister, set them aside to plant in your garden. It's easy to grow plants from dried fruit and vegetable seeds. Get growing!

get ready

Seeds

Patch of yard or planting containers, like flowerpots or yogurt cups

Good dirt

Big spoon or trowel

Pencil

Marker and sticks

Water and watering can

get set

How hard:

How long:

How many:
I or more

Terrain:

get going!

1. Collect seeds from your kitchen and let them dry out. Besides watermelon and squash seeds, try dried lentils and beans, popping corn, and seeds from fresh tomatoes, lemons, and oranges.

2. Prepare the soil. If you are planting seeds in the ground, pick a warm, sunny spot that doesn't flood when it rains. Make sure the soil isn't packed down too hard. If it is, break it up with a sturdy spoon. If you are using containers, fill them with commercial potting soil or dirt from the yard.

3. Water the soil before you plant your seeds, so you don't risk washing the seeds away. Soil should be moist, but not soaking wet.

4. Plant the seeds. Start with more seeds than you want to grow. They probably won't all sprout, and if they do, you can thin the crop, leaving only the strongest plants and weeding out the rest.

5. Set each seed on top of the soil and poke it down under the dirt, using a pencil. Only plant one kind of crop in an area or pot.

6. With a marker, write down the kind of seed you've planted on a little stick and push it into the dirt. These can be "craft" sticks, which are like what's used in popsicles, or "planting" sticks, which are often made of thin plastic. Put your container garden in a sunny spot.

7. Check your garden every day. Keep the soil moist and watch for your first sprouts. Depending on the kind of seed, they may take a few days or a few weeks.

8. If you take good care of your plants and have a bit of luck, you will be able to harvest a snack that you grew yourself.

hot tip

If you decide to start your seeds in containers, bring them inside when the weather gets cold, so they don't freeze.

Want to grow a plant without any seeds? Try planting bulbs, like onions and garlic cloves, and the tops of root vegetables, like carrots and beets. You can even grow plants without dirt—just stick the top of a carrot or yam in a shallow jar of water and watch what happens.

now what?

When preparing the dirt, add your own homemade dirt to the mix as fertilizer (see pages 74–75).

Nature paper

Most paper is made from pulpwood fibers, just like the ones in grass.
So grab a handful of lawn, then pound and pour yourself a page.

get ready

Grass

Block of scrap wood

Hammer or croquet mallet

Boiling water (optional)

Paper

Blender

Large shallow bowl

Flowers and leaves

Mesh, frame, and stapler

Blotter paper, towel, and sponge

get set

How hard:

How long:

How many:

1 or more

Terrain:

get going!

1. Collect a few handfuls of grass. Try long, tough stems from the parts of the lawn where someone forgot to mow—they have extra-long, strong fibers that make good paper.

2. Break down the fibers in the grass. Put your plants on a block of scrap wood to keep from damaging the surface you're working on, or from pounding them into the dirt. Start by pounding the grass with a heavy hammer or mallet. You can loosen the fibers even more by dunking them in boiling water first.

3. Rip up a few sheets of scrap paper into little specks of confetti. The paper fibers will help smooth out the natural ones.

4. Get permission, then throw the grass and confetti into a blender. Ask for help. Mix in about 3 parts water for every part of grass and paper. Don't fill the blender more than $^3/_4$ full, or it will slosh grassy water all over the place. Blend the fibers into a smooth, mushy pulp. The smoother it is, the more it will seem like normal paper. Leave a few blades and stems of grass in a chunky state to give the paper a homemade look.

5. Pour the pulp into a large, shallow bowl that's $^2/_3$ full of water.

6. Find some mesh—the plastic kind used for embroidery, or a window screen, or cheesecloth. Staple the mesh to a picture frame or fit it into an embroidery frame. You can also use the mesh without stapling it. The frame should be small enough to fit into the container of pulp. Your paper will be the size of the mesh.

7. Stir the pulpy water with your hand to get all the fibers suspended in the water. Dip the frame into the container and pull it up so that it fills with the pulp and water. Shake the mesh so that the fibers settle evenly. Sprinkle a few small flowers or leaves over the pulp for a natural effect.

8. If the pulp seems too thick, rinse the fibers back into the water and remove some pulp from the mixture. If not enough fibers cover the entire mesh, make and add more pulp, and dip the frame again.

9. Let the water drain out of the pulp. Set up a piece of blotting paper on a towel. Heavy-weight watercolor paper works well, or, in a pinch, you can use several layers of paper towel. Flip the frame over so that your paper pulp settles on the blotting paper. Set another piece of blotting paper over the pulp, and use a sponge to gently blot up some of the excess water. Allow your new homemade sheet of paper to air dry overnight.

hot tip

Another method is to leave the mesh on the table or the ground, and scoop out the pulp with your hands. Spread it onto the mesh so that it becomes as flat and thin as possible. If you have a large screen, you can make a few small pieces instead of one big one.

now what?

Glue a sheet of your homemade paper into your Nature Scrapbook (see pages 72–73).

JOIN THE BIRDS, *trees, and clouds by sending up a kite to be your eyes. See the world like a bird, then swoop down to sample seed from your homemade feeder. Measure the rain, tell time with the sun, and GET OUT of the way as the wind blows tunes on your chimes. Just remember, when you close your eyes-in-the-sky, you'd better look for unplanned landings!*

Air Crafts

Air Crafts

Engaging rain gauge

Everybody talks about the weather, but nobody does anything about it.
Now you can be the first kid on your block with your own weather station.

get ready

Clear jar with straight sides

Scissors, paper, ruler

Waterproof marker or masking tape

Glue stick

Clear packing tape

Notebook

get set

How hard:

How long:

How many:

1 or more

Terrain:

get going!

1. Find a flat spot to work on, like a picnic table or a level spot in the lawn.

2. Remove any labels from your jar. Make sure the sides are straight, all the way from the top to the bottom. It is important for the opening, where the rain enters, to be the same size as the bottom of the jar, where the rainfall is measured.

3. Make a rainfall scale. Cut a strip of paper a few inches wide and line it up with the edge of a ruler. Mark the scale of inches on the paper with a waterproof marker. White or tan masking tape also works well.

4. Line the scale up with the side of the jar, starting at the bottom. Use a seam in the jar as a guide. Stick the scale in place with the glue stick, then cover it neatly with clear tape to protect the paper from the rain it is measuring.

5. Place your rain gauge in a spot on your patio or in your yard where rain falls straight from the sky. Don't put it up against any walls and stay out from under trees.

6. Wait for rain. In the meantime, start a weather journal in a notebook. Write down what the weather looks like: cloudy or sunny, windy or calm? What time does the sun rise and set? How much rain has fallen?

7. To check on rainfall, wait until the end of a rainstorm, then look at your rain gauge. You can also just check the gauge every day at the same time. Hold the gauge at eye level and read how many inches of water it holds. Empty the gauge, ready for the next rainfall.

8. Keep your rainfall journal current and try to spot patterns. Do rainy days come in bunches? Some people say it rains more on the weekends when they want to be outside than during the week when they are busy with school or work. Is that true? What was the wettest month in your town this year?

hot tip

Having trouble finding a container you can see through that also has straight sides? Try jars that used to hold peanut butter, or jelly, or salsa.

Kite flight delight

Get in touch with your inner Ben Franklin. Make a kite simply from paper and drinking straws, then send it up to fly high in the sky.

get ready

11-by-17-inch piece of paper

Ruler and pencil

Scissors

White glue

Cellophane tape

Hole punch

2 plastic drinking straws

Ribbon

Kite string

get set

How hard:

How long:

How many:

1 or more

Terrain:

get going!

1. You can make this kite with all kinds of paper. Tissue paper is lightweight but flimsy. Heavier craft paper is sturdy, but won't fly without a strong breeze. Ordinary photocopying paper works great. Start with a piece of paper that measures 11 by 17 inches.

2. Fold the paper in half lengthwise, and mark two lines, each ¹/₂ inch from the centerline. Unfold the paper and then, following diagram 1, cut out the shape of the kite. Fold the kite in half again, and fold the wings back along the dotted lines. Glue the body together.

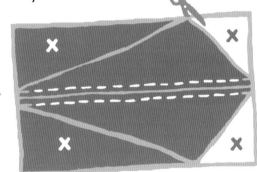

diagram 1

3. Use the small triangles cut from the top of the paper to make the keel. Glue the longest side of the triangles to the body, with the shortest side facing the top of the kite, just like what you see in diagram 2. Glue the triangles together and reinforce the tip of the keel with a piece of cellophane tape. Punch a hole through the keel for the flying line.

keel

diagram 2

4. Make a 10-inch cross spar from the drinking straws. Cut two straws to 5 inches. Take another straw and cut 2 inches off it. Slit the 2-inch section open, so you can wrap it around the longer pieces like a hot dog roll or a burrito. Put one end of each 5-inch straw inside the "wrapper" so that they meet in the middle, and then tape the

diagram 3

ribbons →

whole assembly together. It should now total 10 inches. Tape the spar to the back of the kite sail so that it lines up with the corners. See diagram 3.

5. Tape a piece of ribbon to the bottom point of the kite for a tail. Tie the flying line to the hole in the keel, then go fly a kite.

FLYING TIPS

Start with the kite on the ground or have a friend hold it above her or his head. When the breeze catches the kite, tug on the flying line to gain height. Let the kite pull the string out as it gains altitude. If it starts to dive, let the rope go slack and the kite should even out.

SAFETY NOTE: Don't ever fly a kite near electric power lines or where it could hurt anyone else in falling. Letting it smash into trees, street lights, and walls isn't too bright, either.

hot tip

Make your kite into an art project by decorating it with vivid colors and wild designs.

Big, big bubble machine

You want good, clean fun? Nothing is cleaner—or "gooder"—than a homemade soap-bubble factory. Here's how to blow the biggest bubbles ever in your own giant bubble maker.

get ready

Dishwashing soap, water, and bucket

Glycerin, sugar, corn syrup, or gelatin (optional)

Twine or string and scissors

Drinking straws

get set

How hard:

How long:

How many:

1 or more

Terrain:

get going!

1. Make a batch of bad-tasting bubble juice in a bucket by mixing 1 measure of soap to 10 to 20 measures of water. Sudsier soap and drier days both require more water.

2. To make bubbles so sturdy they bounce, add glycerin (available at a drug store), sugar, corn syrup, or gelatin to the mix. Start with about a tablespoon of any of these for every cup of bubble juice.

3. Build your giant bubblemaker. Cut a piece of heavy twine or cotton kite string about 3 feet long. Thread it through two drinking straws and tie a knot to form a loop. If you are using the bendy kind of straws, cut off the ends that bend.

4. Dip the loop in the bucket of bubble juice. Using the straws as handles, open the loop and blow gently on the soap film. Squeeze the loop shut to help form a complete bubble. If you swirl the bubble maker in the air, you will get funny-shaped bubbles.

Wow! Now you've got a bubble factory!

hot tip

You can even blow bubbles with your bare hands. While your friends are trying the giant bubblemaker, make a circle with your fingers (like the finger sign for "okay"), and dip it in the bubble juice. You should be able to blow bubbles from the soapy film inside the circle. For giant-sized handmade bubbles, dip both hands and make a big circle with your thumbs and pointer fingers.

Jingly wind chime

People use wind power to do all kinds of things: turn windmills, sail sailboats, and blow bubbles using just a blowing breeze. You can harness the power of the wind to make beautiful music, too. It's a breeze!

get ready

Hanger (try a coat hanger, paper towel tube, or thin stick of wood)

Clangers (any small items that make a clanging noise when they bang together)

Ruler

Ties (kitchen twine, embroidery thread, or fishing line)

get set

How hard:

How long:

How many:

I or more

Terrain:

get going!

1. Find a level spot to work on, like a driveway, sidewalk, or picnic table.

2. Lay the hanger down in front of you. The hanger is horizontal and the ties are vertical.

3. With the ruler, measure how long each tie needs to be. First tie it onto the hanger, then pass it through the hole in the clanger and tie a knot. Decide if you want all the clangers to hang evenly, or if you want there to be some pattern to the way they hang.

4. Beginning in the middle of the hanger and working your way out to both edges, tie each clanger to the hanger. They need to be about $^1/_2$ inch apart for them to make music in a gentle wind.

5. To attach each clanger, tie a piece of string to the hanger, and then tie the clanger to the other end of the string. Make sure the string is long enough to let the clangers swing freely.

6. Make sure you check every once in a while to see whether the wind chime is balanced. Adjust the distance between clangers slightly to make up for any imbalance.

7. Once you've got all the clangers attached, it's time to hang the wind chime. If you used a cardboard tube or a stick as a hanger, cut a piece of string and tie it to the ends of the hanger to make a loop for hanging the chime.

8. Find a spot where the breeze blows and where you will be able to hear the chime clanging. Hang it outside a window, from the beam of a porch, or from a low branch near your picnic table.

9. Just sit back, wait for a breezy day, and let the wind make your chime play you a tune. The radio may be quicker, but not as satisfying.

hot tips

- If the clangers are sliding out of place, just attach strips of adhesive tape to the hanger to lock them in place, or make notches in the cardboard of the hanger.

- Choose materials that mean something special to you—a wind chime made from driftwood and seashells makes a great souvenir of your trip to the beach. If you've just moved to a new town, use keys from your old house. You can also use forks and spoons, coins, and nuts and bolts. But don't use anyone's false teeth.

now what?

Got any nuts and bolts left over from making your wind chime? Use them to make a **Fortified Fort** (see pages 66–67).

If you have made a **Rain Gauge** (see pages 84–85), you can add a wind chime to your "weather station."

Bird feeder

If you feed them, they will come. Birds flock to a backyard feeder, come rain or shine, especially if you fill it with nuts and seeds that are for the birds.

get ready

Quart-sized milk carton

Pencil and kitchen knife

Hole punch

Wooden chopstick

Cotton twine

Birdseed or nuts

get set

How hard:

How long:

How many:

1 or more

Terrain:

get going!

1. Wash out the milk carton thoroughly.

2. Make the openings. With a pencil, draw a rectangle 3 inches high by 2½ inches wide on the face of the carton. The bottom of the rectangle should be about 2 inches above the bottom of the carton. Make sure you leave at least ½ inch on either side. Draw the same rectangle on the back face of the carton.

3. Make windows and awnings. Cut out the bottom and sides of the two rectangles, making awnings that hinge on the top.

4. Make the perch. With a hole punch, make a hole underneath each window. Thread a wooden stick through the holes.

5. Open the windows. Punch holes in the ends of the flaps and in the ridge at the top of the carton. Tie a piece of twine between the hole in each flap and the hole in the ridge to keep the flaps pulled open.

6. Prepare to hang the feeder. Tie another loop of string to the ridge hole to use as a loop to hang the feeder.

7. Fill the feeder to the opening. Pick one kind of birdseed or nuts to fill your feeder. If you use a mix, birds will pick through to find their favorites and scatter the seeds they don't like on the ground. Big birds like blue jays prefer sunflower seeds, while smaller birds, like chickadees and finches, prefer peanuts.

8. Place the feeder where you can easily see it, but not so close you'll scare bird visitors away.

diagram 1

diagram 2

diagram 3

now what?

Observe the birds that visit your bird feeder, and draw, photograph, or write about them for your Nature Scrapbook (see pages 72–73).

hot tips

- To feed other kinds of birds, try smearing a bagel or pinecone with peanut butter. Roll in birdseed. Attach string and hang where birds will find it. Yum.

- To make a simple platform feeder, drill drainage holes in a piece of scrap wood and set it up on a pair of bricks. Set out seeds, nuts, and fruit right on the platform.

A timely sundial

Every day, the sun moves across the sky from east to west, casting different shadows. With a sundial, you can use sunny-day shadows and sunbeams to tell the time. And when it's rainy, it's time for an umbrella.

get ready

Poster board, ruler, and scissors

Atlas

Protractor and pencil

Popsicle stick

White glue

Colored markers

Compass

get set

How hard:

How long:

How many:
I or more

Terrain:

get going!

1. Cut a poster board into a 5-inch square.

2. Find out the latitude of where you live. Latitude measures, in degrees, how far you are north or south of the equator. You can find your latitude by looking in an atlas or on the Internet.

diagram 1

3. Using a protractor, measure an angle equal to your latitude in the lower left-hand corner of the square. (See diagram 1.) Mark that angle with an "X." With the pencil, draw a line at that angle from the corner to the opposite side. Mark the same angle in the upper right-hand corner of the square. Cut out both triangles with the scissors.

4. Line up the two triangles with the popsicle stick between them, pointing up from the corner marked "X," and sticking out past the top corner of the triangle. (See diagram 2.) The triangle and popsicle stick are called the gnomon. That's what will tell the time on your sundial.

diagram 2

5. Make the face of the sundial. Cut a poster board into a 12-inch square. Draw a line about 3 inches in from the bottom edge, and put a dot right in the middle. Line the protractor up on the line, centered on the dot. Put a pencil mark every 15 degrees (15, 30, 45, etc.) from 0 to 180, then use a ruler to draw straight lines between the pencil marks and the dot.

6. These lines mark the hours of the day, with the morning on the left and the evening on the right. Starting at 0 degrees (the bottom line), label the intervals 6, 7, 8, 9, 10, 11, 12 (centered at the top), and then 1, 2, 3, 4, 5, and 6. (See diagram 3.)

diagram 3

7. Attach the gnomon to the face of the "clock." The popsicle stick should point up in the air toward the number 12. Cut strips of poster board for supports, and glue the gnomon to the clock. Make sure it is straight up, 90 degrees from the face. (See diagram 4.)

8. Decorate the sundial with dark-colored markers. Make each number a different color, or draw a picture of what you might be doing at each time of the day.

9. Set the dial on the ground in a sunny spot. Find north on a compass, and turn the sundial so that number 12 faces that way. Time to tell time. The shadow of the gnomon falls on the hour of the day. You'll never need a watch again.

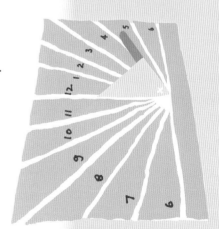

diagram 4

hot tip

The "g" in gnomon isn't pronounced, and "no" is the stressed syllable. Know how to say it now? (No, mon!)

CHIMPANZEES GROOM

each other. Lions lick each other's bellies. Birds bring worms to feed their young. Fish swim in schools to protect each other. The birds and beasties help each other because it's fun, so why don't you? Lend a hand and see what you GET OUT of it. But be sure you get your hand back when you're done!

Helping Hands

Helping Hands

Weeds-be-gone

Weeds look nasty, and they make it hard for "good" plants to grow. Here's how to get the weeds out of your neighborhood—and keep them out—and have fun doing it.

get ready

Gardening gloves and sturdy shoes

Shovels, hoes, spades, and clippers

Wildflower seeds, native plants (optional)

Will power

get set

How hard:

How long:

☀ ☀ ☀

How many:

2 or more

Terrain:

get going!

1. Pick teams and stake out your turf. Each group should choose a corner of someone's overgrown yard, or pick the strips of greenery between the sidewalk and the street. Perhaps there's a vacant lot or part of a public park that could use your attention.

2. Set a time limit for the clean-up phase of the battle. Each side will have that much time for their weeds to be gone.

3. Wear gloves and sturdy shoes while you pull, dig, chop, twist, and hoe every weed you see.

   Note: Weeds are plants that people don't want in their gardens or lawns—what's a flower or food for one person may be a weed for another (think dandelions). Ask for help in identifying which plants are weeds before you start wiping every growing thing off the face of the earth, especially if you are working near someone's garden.

4. When time's up, get together to see which team has done the best job of weeding their area. (This is the kind of game that everybody wins, because the grounds will look so much better, no matter what.)

5. If you want to keep the weeds out for good, plant wildflowers, grasses, and vines that are native to your area. Your local garden club or parks department can help you decide what to plant. If you explain to the local gardening store that you're trying to clean up your neighborhood, it might even donate seeds or plants, especially if you offer to put up a sign thanking the store for its support.

now what?

Litter is a common bedfellow to weeds. Picking it up is always part of gardening. To try litter picking on its own, turn to pages 106–107.

hot tip

"Green" debris can usually be recycled, as can lots of litter, like bottles, cans, and newspapers. Just one more way to Save the Planet!

Beautify a park

Do you wish your local playground or park were kept in better condition? It's your park, it's your playground, so why not fix it up yourself?

get ready

Work gloves

Rakes, brooms, and lawn mower

Trash bags

Paintbrushes and paint

Hammer and nails

get set

How hard:

How long:

How many:
1 or more

Terrain:

get going!

1. Survey the site and see what's needed. Does the lawn need mowing? Do the leaves need raking? Is there lots of litter? Do the benches need a coat of paint, or are they falling apart? Make a list of all the work that needs to be done.

2. Very important: Get permission from whoever's in charge. Call the parks department, the office of public works, or the school board, and let them know that you want to help.

3. Organize a work crew. Ask your friends or even your parents— just don't let them forget they're working for you. If you're planning to do any complicated work, like carpentry or painting, make sure someone in your group is an expert, so he or she can show the others what to do.

4. Collect the necessary tools and supplies. If you don't have them all on hand, ask friends, parents, or local contractors to let you borrow tools and supplies for your project.

now what?

Just in case the park authorities don't like your ideas, try cleaning up your neighborhood instead (see pages 106–107).

If you have a Lawn Care business (see pages 120–121), volunteering to clean up the neighborhood park can be great publicity.

Pack a Picnic (see pages 34–35) and make the most of your break time.

5. Prioritize and plan. Estimate how long the work will take, and bring snacks and beverages if you will be there for more than an hour or two.

6. Get to work.

hot tip

Something missing from a park or a playground you use? Do you wish there were hiking trails, a bike path, or a skateboard area? Why not build it? Get organized, develop plans, get permission, get help, and make it happen.

Help a neighbor

Have you done a good deed today? How about this week?
(This month??) Why not find someone who needs a hand,
and help him or her out?

get ready

A kind heart and
a little time

get set

How hard:

How long:

How many:
1 or more

Terrain:

get going!

1. Some folks have a hard time getting all the things done that they need to do, often because they just don't have the time or the energy. Think of someone you know who you think could use your help.

2. Ask what you can do to help out. Make a specific offer: If you know your neighbor is having a hard time getting to the grocery store because he hurt his leg, offer to do the shopping for him. Does the couple next door with the new baby have trouble finding time to clean their house? Offer to watch the baby in their yard. (You could clean the house, but playing with the baby would probably be more fun.) There are plenty of little chores and errands you can do to make your neighbors' lives just a little easier: mowing their lawn, shoveling their snow, or walking their dog.

3. If people tell you they don't need any help, respect their independence. Remember the old saying, "Some kinds of help are the kinds of help that helping's all about, and some kinds of help are the kinds of help we all can do without."

now what?

Do you have a Kid Business (see pages 112–125)? Helping out can be great publicity. Potential paying customers may be impressed with the good job you are doing while you are performing your good deeds.

hot tip

You might even want to try out this activity on your parents!

Litter pickup

Have a contest to see who's the quicker litter picker-upper. Grab grungy gunk to win goodies. Think of it as the world's grossest treasure hunt. The grand prize is a cleaner neighborhood.

get ready

Gloves

Garbage bags

Shovel, pointy stick, and broom

get set

How hard:

How long:

How many:

2 or more

Terrain:

get going!

1. Set boundaries and time limits for the contest. Clean up your whole block or concentrate on one especially yucky spot.

2. Pick categories for prizes. See who can fill the most bags and who can find the oldest, biggest, and grossest pieces of trash. Give a special prize to anyone who can find a piece of litter in all the colors of the rainbow.

3. Decide what the prizes are: loser takes out the trash at home for a month, or winner gets to keep the refund money from returning deposit bottles and cans.

4. Start picking. Wear gloves if you are handling trash other than loose paper blowing on the street.

5. Contestants should stack their garbage bags in separate piles. Set aside recyclables and returnable bottles, and put things in separate bags that you think might win a prize in one of the special categories.

6. Dig, jab, and sweep that trash into submission.

7. When time is up, gather together to see who won, and to give out prizes.

now what?

Keep an eye out for good junk that you can use, like scrap wood for building a **Fortified Fort** (pages 66–67) or clangers for making a **Jingly Wind Chime** (pages 90–91).

hot tip

One fair way to measure litter is to weigh the bags. Stand on a bathroom scale empty handed, then pick up your bags of trash. The difference between the before and after poundage is the weight of your trash.

Plant an oasis

A bright dash of color from sidewalk flowers can warm the heart, and nothing refreshes the soul like the shade of a tree on a hot summer's day. Plant an oasis to share with your whole neighborhood.

get ready

Gardening gloves

Watering can or hose

Shovel, trowel, and other gardening tools, as needed

Young trees, shrubs, seedlings, or seeds

get set

How hard:

How long:

How many:

I or more

Terrain:

get going!

1. Find a spot that needs flowers or a tree, like an empty dirt patch between the squares of a sidewalk or a weedy stretch by the side of a road. Get permission to plant there.

2. Learn what kinds of plants will do well in the spot that you've picked. Ask an expert gardener, the city parks department, or a local nursery. Some plants survive better or are more suited than others in harsh environments. (Some cities will donate a street tree, if you promise to take care of it.)

3. Prepare the soil for planting. This step can be messy; you'll want to wear gardening gloves. Dig out any weeds you find, loosen the soil with a trowel or shovel, and moisten it to make a nice, comfortable home for the plants to move into. Mix some ground-up vegetable scraps into the soil. As they rot, they will provide nutrients for your plant to feed on.

4. Dig a hole that's slightly larger than the plants you want to put into the ground. Now the only trick is to put the green side up and the brown side down. Fill in plenty of soil around each plant, mashed down firmly so it doesn't wiggle around. If you are planting seeds, follow the instructions on the package.

5. Take care of anything you plant as it grows. Pull out any weeds that appear, and make sure the soil stays moist. You can also water greenery that you didn't plant; it will be most appreciative.

hot tip

One fair way to measure litter is to weigh the bags. Stand on a bathroom scale empty handed, then pick up your bags of trash. The difference between the before and after poundage is the weight of your trash.

Collect for charity

One kid's cast-off ski jacket might be another kid's only warm coat. If your neighborhood's hand-me-downs have nowhere to go, collect them and share them with a local charity.

get going!

1. Pick a charity that does work that feels important to you. Ask your friends, your parents, your school, or a local church to suggest a good organization. You can check with the better business bureau in your town to make sure the charity is really a worthy one.

2. Give toys for the holidays, warm coats before a cold winter sets in, or whatever is needed whenever you can.

3. Get a big group together. The more people you can get involved, the more help you can provide together.

4. Make a plan for your collection drive. You could go door to door to your neighbors, or put up signs around the block (or around town) asking for donations to be dropped off at a specific time and place.

5. Make your collecting fun for everyone. Sing a song or do a dance routine in exchange for a donation, or hand out little prizes, like stickers or pieces of candy.

THERE'S NO BUSINESS

like kid business, like no business you know. You have the corner on the market, so why not make a market on the corner? Your lemonade is the sweetest. Your neighbors' pets like you the most. And, let's face it, your prices are the best. Here are some ideas for going into business for yourself. So GET OUT your thinking cap and make cents out of sense.

Kid Business

Kid Business

Lemonade stand

Thirsty people everywhere, and not enough to drink. Make a mint selling cool, refreshing lemonade.

get ready

Lemons, sugar, salt, and water

Water and ice, and more lemons

Cutting board, knife, lemon squeezer, grater, and measuring cups (dry and wet)

Pitchers or jars for lemon syrup and water, ice holder, paper cups

Paper and markers for signs

Table and chairs

Box with lid for change and money

get set

How hard:

How long:

How many:
1 or more

Terrain:

get going!

1. Get your recipe down. Test it on friends and family, and develop a lemonade (or other drink) that people really like. (Try out the sample recipe shown here for starters.)

2. Calculate how much each serving costs, and make sure you charge enough to cover them. Remember that part of the cost is the amount of time it takes you to mix up a batch, so pay yourself fairly for your time. Find out how much stores nearby charge for their drinks to see if your price is reasonable.

3. Study your market. When do the most people walk by? When do they seem the thirstiest? Set your stand up to meet peak demand. Do you live near a popular bike path or jogging route? Exercise builds a powerful thirst. Are construction workers building something on your block? Make sure you are set up for their lunch break. Is there a parade coming up? All those spectators are potential customers.

Lemonade

Here's our favorite drink recipe.

To make lemonade syrup:

2 cups sugar

1 cup water

Rind of 2 well-washed lemons, grated

$\frac{1}{8}$ teaspoon salt

Juice of 6 lemons

Stir sugar, water, grated lemon rind, and salt in a pan over medium heat for 5 minutes. Cool and add lemon juice. Strain through a mesh strainer and store in a pitcher or jar.

To serve:

Add 2 tablespoons lemonade syrup to a glass of ice water. Stir. Garnish with a wedge of fresh lemon.

Makes about 12 servings.

4. Set up your table and hang signs advertising your lemonade. Let people see the fresh lemons, so they know you are offering them a high-quality product. Cut wedges of lemon on the spot to add to each cup of lemonade that you sell, so it looks as fresh as it can be.

5. Have a supply of quarters, nickels, and dimes on hand, so you can make change for your customers. It's also easier to keep track of the money if you have a box or container with a lid to keep it in.

6. Ask your customers how well they like your lemonade. Keep refining the recipe until it looks the best it can be.

hot tips

- Once your lemonade stand is famous far and wide, sell your recipe to the restaurants around town.

- Offer to provide lemonade for birthday parties and picnics in the neighborhood.

- Also sell food with your lemonade, like cookies or cupcakes.

Pet care

If you love animals, taking care of other people's pets can really pay off.

get going!

1. Tell people that you are starting a pet care business. Convince them that you are responsible. Offer to walk their dog after school or to feed and pet their pets while they are away on vacation.

2. Write the name of your company on a T-shirt or baseball cap with a colorful marker, and wear it while you are working. That way, people will know you are a professional, and not just out for a stroll with your own dog.

3. Make sure you clean up after any dog you are walking. Hold onto a plastic bag and turn it inside out, pick up the poop, and turn the bag outside in. Twist and knot the top of the bag and dump it.

4. Know the dog's leash habits, and learn how to keep a dog under control. Some professional dog walkers walk many, many dogs at once, but this is probably not a good idea. Walk one dog at a time, and add more only if you (and the dog) are still having fun.

5. Lots of pets just need to be checked on. Cats and dogs need to have water and food, and they need affection and attention. They may need to be scratched and have a ball thrown for them. Cat- and dogsitting is a service that the pets will love.

6. Learn as much as you can about animals: Study biology, read books on raising and training animals, and talk to the experts. Your customers will appreciate your knowledge.

7. Do a great job. The best way to get more business is to get referrals from satisfied customers.

now what?

Organize a Blue-Ribbon Pet Show (pages 42–43) to publicize your services. It's a great way to meet all the animal lovers in the neighborhood. They're not just potential customers, they're potential friends.

hot tip

Once you've mastered the art of walking, feeding and watering, and playing with pooches and putty-tats, why not learn how to wash and brush them and cut their hair? Animal grooming is a booming business.

Lawn care

There are acres and acres of lawn in America—someone's got to mow them.

get ready

Lawn mower

Gardening tools

Wood and paint

get set

How hard:

How long:

How many:

1 or more

Terrain:

get going!

1. Start by doing a fantastic job taking care of your yard at home. When the lawn and garden look perfect, paint a sign on a scrap of wood that says "Professional Lawn Care by My Lawncare Company" (make up a name for your own company). Offer to keep your lawn at home in tip-top shape in exchange for the use of the family mower and other gardening equipment, until you can afford to buy your own.

2. Start asking your neighbors for work. The pros call it landscaping, and it's not just cutting grass. Watering the garden, weeding, caring for trees, and cleaning up leaves are all part of the job. Be flexible and many opportunities will come to you.

3. Figure out how much you need to charge in order to make a profit. Consider all the costs: gasoline, equipment, repairs, garbage bags, and your time. Weigh your expenses: Is it better to spend money on gas for a fast lawn mower or to spend time cutting grass with a hand-pushed model? As long as you are making a profit on each job, you will earn more and more money as you get more business.

4. Before mowing, check the yard to make sure there are no sticks or rocks that could get caught in the mower's blades and become lawn-mower missles. Wear long pants and sturdy shoes, and make sure you follow all of the safety instructions for each piece of equipment that you use.

5. Talk to your clients about how they want their lawn mowed. Do they want a trim, 1-inch cut, or something a little longer and more natural looking? Do they want you to bag or rake the trimmings, or would they prefer you leave them on the lawn as natural fertilizer?

now what?

Publicize your business by doing volunteer work in the neighborhood. You might mow an elderly neighbor's lawn for free (see **Help a Neighbor**, pages 104–105) and leave your sign on the lawn while you work, clean all the weeds out of a vacant lot (see **Weeds-Be-Gone**, pages 100–101), or plant flowers and trees beside the sidewalk on your block (see pages 108–109). Let people know that your company has donated its services for these worthy causes.

6. Taking care of a lawn is more than just mowing. Lawns need to be watered, fertilized, and aerated. Learn about the specific needs of lawns in the area where you live, and offer a full-service package to your customers.

7. The best way to get more business is to do excellent work. That way, your customers will ask you to come back, and they may refer you to other people who need your services.

Door-to-door car wash

With a little business sense, you can really clean up at the car wash.

get ready

Bucket, soap, and water

Hose

Sponges, squeegee, towels

get set

How hard:

How long:

How many:

1 or more

Terrain:

get going!

1. Before you become a car washer, you need customers. Ask the folks who live on your block. Your two best bets for customers are those with really yucky-looking cars that need a wash bad and those with really nice cars who know how important it is to take care of them.

2. Offer to do the work right away or to schedule a time that's convenient for them. Show up on time for your appointment.

3. Organize all of your equipment and supplies in a bucket, so that you are always ready to do a job, and don't need to fumble around in the closet and cupboard looking for soap and sponges every time you want to wash a car. Figure out how much your soap and sponges cost per car wash, and charge enough to cover your expenses and pay yourself for your time.

4. Develop a car-washing system that works well for you: If you are working alone, you may want to work on one part of the car at a time, wetting, soaping, and rinsing piece by piece. If you are part of a team, one person can operate the hose, while the others soap and scrub and dry. Be careful to rinse all the soap off before it dries, or it will leave spots and streaks. Work quickly, but carefully.

5. Cut down on the time between jobs by scheduling sequential appointments for people who live near one another. Ride your bike between appointments. The more work you can get done in a short period of time, the higher your profits will be.

6. Do a great job for your customers. Ask when they would like you to come back, and tell them to let their friends know that you're available to wash their cars, too.

Become an all-purpose transportation cleaner-upper: Ask your friends if they need their bikes washed.

hot tip

"Detailing" is an extension of car washing, and covers vacuuming the inside of a car and waxing the outside till it shines. It takes lots more time, because it's all in the details.

Yard sale

Set up a bizarre bazaar to sell your odds and ends.

get ready

Sale items

Paper and markers, or chalk

Tape and pen

Box with lid for change and money

get set

How hard:

How long:

How many:

1 or more

Terrain:

get going!

1. Decide what you want to sell. Do you have clothes, toys, or books that you have outgrown? Have you been building a comic book collection that you're ready to start selling off?

2. Organize a block-wide or neighborhood-wide sale, or schedule your sale to coincide with a sale that's already planned. Multiple yard sales draw more customers.

3. Advertise to attract customers. Make signs with markers and tape them up around the block, or write signs on the sidewalk with chalk. If you are planning to have a big sale, it might be worth taking out an ad in the newspaper.

4. Offer to sell other folks' stuff for a percentage of the sales. Does your dad have a collection of snazzy clothes from the 1970s hidden away in the closet?

5. Decide what your merchandise is worth. Write prices on tape and label each item, or offer groups of items for the same price. Rule of thumb: If the stuff sells fast, the prices may be too low; if it sells slow, the prices may be too high.

6. Be friendly to customers, but don't crowd them. Let them browse, and be prepared to bargain if someone offers you a lower price than what you've marked on an item. In fact, always be ready to go lower—people love discounts!

now what?

At the end of the sale, pack up the stuff you haven't sold and take it to a charitable organization (see pages 110–111).

Combine your yard sale with other special events, like an Art Show (see pages 58–59). Your customers will "get some culture," and these same art lovers may end up buying something from your sale.

hot tip

Become an expert in a particular specialty. If you really love dolls, you could start going to flea markets and other people's yard sales to check out the prices and see what people like to collect. Read price guides and histories to learn more about your specialty. As you become familiar with the market, you can start collecting dolls of your own to sell at future yard sales. There's one simple rule: buy low, sell high. As long as you are able to do that, you'll come out ahead. Also, if you pick a subject that you really enjoy, and like to talk to the folks you are buying and selling from, your business will feel more like fun than work.

Index

About the creators...

Orange Avenue creates a wide variety of books for young readers. For more information about Orange Avenue and its products, go to www.orangeavenue.com.

Hallie Warshaw, Orange Avenue's owner and creative director, loves children's books and bright colors. Hallie has created lots of books for children. One of the experiences that has influenced her most was being an arts-and-crafts counselor at Lake Farm summer camp in Cape Cod. She lives in San Francisco in a pastel blue building that she wishes were painted bright orange.

Jake Miller writes for kids and adults about science and culture. He is also a photographer and filmmaker, and a kite test pilot. He lives in Boston with his wife, who has been very understanding about the messes he makes while developing experiments and art projects.

Julie Brown, a freelance photographer who lives in San Francisco, loves to photograph people, and this is her second book for children. Julie also specializes in black-and-white documentary photography. She holds a Bachelor of Fine Arts from Rochester Institute of Technology.

Madeleine Budnick gets out as often as she can. Raised on stoopball and freeze tag in the wilds of Yonkers, New York, she now lives in Northern California and avoids pavement whenever possible. While she has designed many, many books for children, these are her first published illustrations.